ROB2

Songs from the Hills

Songs from the Hills

AN INTIMATE LOOK AT COUNTRY MUSIC

MARIA VON MATTHIESSEN

MACMILLAN PUBLISHING COMPANY
NEW YORK
MAXWELL MACMILLAN CANADA
TORONTO
MAXWELL MACMILLAN INTERNATIONAL
NEW YORK   OXFORD   SINGAPORE   SYDNEY

Macmillan Publishing Company
866 Third Avenue
New York, NY 10022

Maxwell Macmillan Canada, Inc.
1200 Eglinton Avenue East
Suite 200
Don Mills, Ontario M3C 3N1

Macmillan Publishing Company is part of the
Maxwell Communication Group of Companies.

Frontispiece: Landscape, Murfreesboro Hills, Tennessee

Library of Congress Cataloging-in-Publication Data
Von Matthiessen, Maria.
    Songs from the hills: an intimate look at country music / by Maria von Matthiessen.
        p.   cm.
    ISBN 0-02-581850-3
    1. Country music—History and criticism. 2. Country music—Pictorial works. I. Title.
    ML3524.V66   1993
    781.642—dc20   93-23906   CIP   MN

Macmillan books are available at special discounts for bulk purchases for sales promotions, premiums, fund-raising, or educational use. For details, contact:

Special Sales Director
Macmillan Publishing Company
866 Third Avenue
New York, NY 10022

Design by Janet Tingey

10 9 8 7 6 5 4 3 2 1

PRINTED IN THE UNITED STATES OF AMERICA

In the heart of every true artist
there comes the cry,
Give me the chance to do my very best.

—ACHILLE PAPIN

And no less happy he who knows the rural gods.

—VIRGIL

This book is dedicated to the Tennessee land—and its simple dignity. It will survive even if you do not go out and embrace it—it will still be there—able to comfort itself quietly, content to *just be*. This is its message.

INTRODUCTION

THERE WAS A FIELD behind the house where I grew up about seventy miles north of New York City. It was the second field up, a wide, upward-sloping field edged on four sides with piles of rounded rocks made into walls. There was a fine view from up there of distant hills covered with maple and oak and elm.

As a child I would bring my favorite books to this field, dragging an old coat along behind me to scrunch up against a special rock sticking up from the ground near the top of the hill. Then I would lean back and look out at the distant hills and think, while shooing away an occasional bug with a swisher, a small branch I would tear off from a tree as I came up through the fields.

The ground was especially comforting in this field too. Why, I don't know. It just seemed to be a particularly happy field, and even in the summer heat its warmth beneath me calmed me. I was always especially grateful for its last warming touch in the late autumn when I would snuggle up in an old coat as the cold winds began to blow up the hill—soon to be singing their lonely winter songs above the still ground covered with slush and ice.

I do not go to that field anymore. The land has been sold to a developer, and, over the years, my life as a photographer has taken me to many faraway fields where I seemed to no longer want to look at distant hills, but inward, inside the great *schlosses* of the Schoenborns and Metternichs in Austria and Germany for *Town and Country* magazine in the seventies and inside the humongous, architecturally imitative somethings in Texas, and inside the unexpectedly simple and "normal" homes of Jimmy Stewart and Dionne Warwick and others in Los Angeles during the eighties. All of this inward viewing of people's lifestyles has been a part of twenty-or-so years of chronicling different societies visually. This chronicling began in 1972 when I went to visit the late great British chronicler of society, Sir Cecil Beaton, at his London flat in

Fulham, to do my first assignment for *Town and Country*, a piece on "Those Imaginative Green Thumbs"—English gardeners.

I arrived at the front door of Sir Cecil's flat, and was greeted by his personal aide, a quiet young man wearing a dark suit, who guided me to a crimson velvet chair in the little sitting room to the left. There I was placed to await Sir Cecil's descent from a room somewhere upstairs.

I remember leaning anxiously forward, barely breathing, so I could listen carefully for Sir Cecil's footsteps upon the stairs and be ready within myself for his entrance. I was still young and could, at times, be monumentally apprehensive.

When Sir Cecil finally appeared, preceded by his aide, he was resplendent in an impeccably cut double-breasted gray flannel suit contoured at the waist and slightly flared at the hips—his white hair swept up smoothly off his forehead. He held himself quite upright as he looked down at me. I had never before seen such elegance and style in a man.

His presence immediately took over the little sitting room, and we yielded to it completely, as he tossed his hands about in the air, left and right from the wrist, while telling witty stories about this and that—dialogue glazed with an exquisitely fine layer of arrogance.

I had listened to dialogue of this sort before, though not quite so wonderfully British, from writers and other clever, creative people who would come out from New York on weekends to visit my mother, Barbara Heggie, a writer of some profiles for *The New Yorker* and other magazines in the forties. They would come to the pre-Revolutionary War farmhouse that sat at the bottom of the fields I described earlier, and they would stroll about the many tall, still rooms with their occasional creaking old wood floorboards, telling stories, and some would talk while leaning on the mantelpieces of the brick fireplaces that were in every room. In the winter the fireplaces would be lit with crackling wood fires.

I listened carefully to their talk for I seemed to want to know what they would have to say, and I made pictures in my mind from their talk as I walked about after them, listening. They did not seem at all aware of my being there, and I did not seem to have a need to invite any acknowledgment from them for my being there, and so I would just listen for hours until somebody suddenly, with a feeling from out of nowhere, would realize my presence, and the late hour, and I would be led off to bed. It was this growing up in a world of words that made pictures that led me later on to try and make pictures with a camera, visual dialogues, or what I later called "photo-concepts," a telling of a little bit about the subject and his world by taking bits and pieces of things from the room or space about the subject, and then seeking out natural light and shadow where possible, and then considering the form and structure of things, and then bringing this all together while directing the subject for that *moment*.

When I met Sir Cecil, I decided to begin at once a chronicle of society, British society. It was my first visual dialogue, my first attempt at photo-concepts. This endeavor was tied to my own roots, for in growing up isolated on 250 acres of land, way out there somewhere, with nothing around for miles, books became a way for me to entertain myself. There were books everywhere, there was an upstairs bookshelf, a downstairs bookshelf, and a children's bookshelf in my room. (My father was a very cultured European who feared that too much television would drag one down to a level from which one could never again ascend.) The characters that were described in those books I read were ones I felt I wanted to know more about because I was very curious to find out what human beings were all about, and who I was, by measuring myself against them.

In the winter of 1991, I was standing in the field of an old farmer, below Nashville, a field enclosed by tightly stacked and packed slabs of chiseled granite, and I was looking out at distant hills again, this time at the quiet hills of Tennessee. I felt I needed, as Edward Steichen once felt, to find a reaffirmation of life by a returning to nature. I felt I needed to find some higher form of spiritual expression manifesting itself here, apart from the *self*, and I was hoping that this manifestation of a higher form of expression would speak to me up from the Tennessee ground, and down from the Tennessee sky, and out through the wind, and out from the trees. I was hoping that nature would confirm the need for an essential order and discipline, *here*. My thought was to do my next chronicle on country music singers so that I might combine them with nature. I have always felt that country music was a unique part of the American cultural heritage, and that it speaks so eloquently of the essence of America.

So how does one begin a serious photographic study, and with what does one begin? I believe that one begins by standing still and looking into one's state of mind. For whatever the photographer's feelings are about the world, about himself, about everything at that time, is going to give the shape to, and the look of, his creative endeavor. I believe that the spirit/mind energy thinking of that particular time in the photographer's life goes forth to meet the subject during the photo session, and that when the photographer stretches toward his subject, and tries to get the subject to stretch back to him, that an essential part of the photographer transfers over on to the subject.

So there you are beginning your photographic study, standing in the doorway of an empty room, looking in on empty space, and knowing that whatever you place in the room will have a sense of you, and how then do you go out, so to speak, to get your objects to place in that room? Where do you begin, what will you say? The sculptor Henry Moore suggested letting come what comes. Don't come, he advised, with any preconceived ideas. Just allow the work of art to unfold as you go along. It will begin to shape itself in time.

My approach for the first four months of my country music study was to place the singers in a simple space, preferably in their homes, to hear them talk to get a feel and understanding of what I was working with. I made basic portraits as I began, seeking some direction. I borrowed the living room of a kind lady in Belle Meade, a residential district in Nashville, when I did Loretta Lynn. It was not possible to do her at home. She apparently had a number of homes here and there, including several in Hawaii, but there were time constraints, I soon learned, for my photo-sessions. Most of my subjects were passing through Nashville, on their way to their next gig, and each ticking moment was carefully being observed by the publicist and manager and producer, etc., etc., a whole orchestration of people who stood behind each singer.

I did Charlie Daniels at another private home in Nashville, early in the morning. (The owners had a piece of Christo sculpture, the American artist who wraps things—and I wanted to wrap Charlie Daniels in an American flag and lasso, as a piece of American art, next to the Christo.) A huge purple bus came roaring into the driveway, shuddered to a halt—endless antennae swaying from the roof—a large figure rushed from the bus, fidgeted restlessly after the first four minutes (his mind already back on the road), and then leapt hastily for the door when his time was up, and went roaring out of town on his bus, leaving the hostess bug-eyed with fractured nerves, and me quietly grateful.

This constant movement, I soon learned, is an essential part of their profession. Country music is universally popular and the singers travel all over the world, so the few weeks out of every year that they get to spend at home makes it a place that is off-limits to any business activity, and therefore difficult for the photographer to set up a photo-session there.

Loretta Lynn came hurriedly too, into a borrowed living room, followed by her Nashville manager, Louie, and after rushing my eyes from the head to the toe of her, trying to get a point of view in seconds, I beseeched the Belle Meade lady for some white bedsheets, and could I please borrow the little porcelain songbird I saw on her bookshelf by the TV? for I felt in Miss Lynn a childlike spirit and a certain vulnerability in her sweet concern to make us all comfortable with her, to satisfy us with what she felt she was supposed to provide us with, of herself— meeting the expectations of a legendary character, I suppose. I felt that she must exhaust her strength at times with this, for she does not measure herself out carefully, she gives too much. She is a loving, very sensitive person in that way. I wanted to give her a hug to reassure her, but, instead, I sat her on the floor to pose her, while she talked constantly, telling us stories about growing-up times—how her parents carried her twelve miles through the winter cold as a little baby, wrapped in a quilt, trekking through the snow to find a doctor for her ear infection—she showed us the scar behind her ear. At one point she indicated that her throat was dry, and everyone rushed forward to offer a glass of water? juice? No, she said she wanted a piece of chewing gum, only that, she thought would help her dry throat.

So Louie, her manager went hurrying off to get her some, and reappeared shortly with five large packs of everything from cinnamon to Carefree Sugarless Bubble, whereupon Miss Lynn selected a peppermint gum, tearing off a little edge of gum from the stick, just a little corner, and began to discreetly chew.

With the bedsheets I was able to cover the furniture behind Miss Lynn, and with the little bird placed on the bedsheet to the right of her, I hoped to convey that sense of childlike sweetness—quite a nice quality, actually, to find in this rough and tumble going-for-a-buck world of today. She could have been as tough as nails and hard and calculating.

As Louie whisked her out the door, on to her next appointment, she left behind her in the living room a feeling of a sweet, gentle wildflower. She is actually very shy.

My session with Emmylou Harris was a fine photographic experience. We did her in her home, in her large, old white wooden house, somewhere on the outskirts of Nashville. She is a natural beauty, lovely, with lots of thick, dark hair left untouched to go gray. She has pale English skin and high cheekbones. She moved constantly, quick movements everywhere, singing at times to herself, not for our benefit, but just because that's what went through her.

On her way to the kitchen to make tea for us, she passed her guitar standing in the hall, picked it up, and strummed it a little bit, and then put it down and went on, singing to herself in the kitchen while she made tea, singing to the tea tray in the hall as she came back to us in the living room.

Emmylou has unusually long, thin fingers, and I decided to put the attention here and on her lovely face. My two assistants took up a rug of patterned roses from the floor, and tacked it to the mantelpiece behind her, and I used my little artificial light source to highlight her hands and face. We placed my one light low on the floor to the left of her, and tipped the bulb up at her.

My next subject was the smooth-singing Eddy Arnold. I found in his character qualities that I found later on in a lot of the other country music singers. There is little flimflam, little hype, no overdoing. He has a decency about him, a nice politeness, and a reserve too, a slight holding back, much like the Tennessee hills and the Tennessee farmers I went to meet later on to see if

I could use their land for my photo-sessions. I sensed without words spoken that they were happy to just *be,* and that the *being* was not dependent on outside approval and getting things and having things.

I used the dining room table of another lady in Belle Meade, taking all of her neoclassic silver candlesticks and placing them in two rows, running up the table. I sat Mr. Arnold at the end of them. For me the candlesticks represented the simple dignity and style of the man, and in turning off most of the artificial lights in the room, and having candlelight, I hoped to convey a slightly mystical feeling.

By the spring of 1991, I tried to settle down with one unifying point of view. I had met and photographed a number of singers now: "The Outlaw," Waylon Jennings, and his exceptionally kind wife, Jessi Colter; the wiry old birdlike bluegrass legend Bill Monroe (he reminds me on stage of a slender waterfowl stepping lightly from foot to foot in a marsh) in his log cabin looking out on a field of goats; the elegant and tall T.G. Sheppard; the saucy, spunky Tanya Tucker. I began to come up with ideas like, well now, maybe since I want to return to nature, I will try to photograph everyone through a cornstalk root, for the structure was intriguing—many long thin fingers of roots—and there would be the symbolism of the roots of America, from which country music comes, or our need now to return to our roots. But the spirit of the country music singers did not speak a conceptual, more avant-garde point of view, and so the guidance was strong to maintain the more classical, pure vision I had attempted to lay the groundwork with, and to carry it with me, now, out into my exploration of the Tennessee landscape. One of my first sessions out-of-doors was in the spring in the field of an old farmer, Walter Ragsdale, below Nashville, in Brentwood. For many a late spring and summer day thereafter, I would go walk in his field to think about my project and other things. Every time I went there was a different experience of feeling and sound—as I walked through the field of constantly calling crickets. Sometimes there was the sensible, clear call of a bobwhite, usually one at one end of the field, and one at the other, "bobwhite" echoed back with "bobwhite." Other days there would be the slight screeching call of hawks circling overhead, or a pileated woodpecker drilling on a dead part of a tree growing along the granite-slabbed wall—and, soothingly, sometimes the soft cooing of wild pigeons, deep in the woods.

It was the feel and sound of the wind that I liked best, though usually it just ruffled by my ears, down from the small hill across the road (that looked in the deep summer, with its heavily leafed trees, like a fat English tea bun overloaded with sugar), and then it went on past me to the row of trees that ran along the granite wall, turning back their leaves as it ruffled down the row. Several times in the middle of the summer it was very hot, and everything stopped dead, and panted. My favorite day of wind came in August. It came once, and never came again. It was like a sea wind. The way it swayed the leaves made them sound like waves breaking on a shore, and then it came, singing, not ruffling, by my ears as I walked along.

Every week the field yielded something different to see, and it did it calmly in its own time. In the spring there were lots of purple thistles everywhere, and the granite walls were swept with fragrant-smelling honeysuckle. Then came lots of little yellow flowers, and then there were some unusual purple flowers, growing close to the ground, and then, some exquisite tiny white wildflowers at the end of tall, stalked stems, and some equally lovely little white butterflies with wings edged in pale blue would come to alight atop them. Many times I wondered *who* had made all of these shapes and colorings and patterns in nature, those bizarre-looking violet flowers, that little shiny emerald green bee I saw once on a purple flower in the late autumn next to a round little yellow bug with tiny black spots. Where did all these very intricate and precise ideas come from?

I took the young and popular singer Mark Miller, leader of the group Sawyer Brown, to farmer Ragsdale's field, along with one of the members of his group, Greg "Hobbie" Hubbard. I placed them among the leaves and blossoms of early summer dogwood, and tried to speak the gentle late spring magic of that field through them. I asked Mark to sing, as the field sang for me, and for Hobbie, whom I placed to his left, to be quiet and thinking. I put the background out of focus to provide a softer mood. Just as I had wondered where did the visual magic come from in Mr. Ragsdale's field, I wondered where did the musical magic come from in the country music singers? Many of the old timers had had no formal training and little education. Yet when they picked up pieces of wood and bits of string they began to speak special sounds, and from within themselves they would find words to go with these special sounds. Many had sharp wits. I could barely get a sentence out of my mouth with the wonderfully rotund Grand Ole Opry star Johnny Russell. He would come zipping back at me with some clever response. His conversation created a thicket of diverse images like the special verbal/visual experience expressed in country music songs. This witty image-making shaped another point of view for my study, that of whimsical and, at times, metaphorical concepts. Harlan Howard, the legendary songwriter, with decades of hits beginning with Patsy Cline's "I Fall to Pieces," had this quick-minded humor about him, and I tried to make use of this approach with him.

Harlan was an orphan and when he was ten, "a couple of old folks" took him to their farm, "in a little town called Leslie, Michigan. They were paid seven dollars a week by the state, and they sent me to school and somehow or another clothing was provided, and books, and I did the chores.

"They had eight or nine cows and I would be sent out early in the morning to milk the cows, feed the horses, hoe the corn. I'd squirt milk from the cows to the rhythm of an Ernest Tubb song. I heard Ernest Tubb on the Grand Ole Opry radio program, on the Philco radio of the farmer, and it blew my mind. I found the radio on the mantel in the small den, a little old round-top deal, about a foot high, and so one winter night after undressing in front of the pot-bellied stove in the kitchen and going up to my room on the second floor (boy it was howling up there, it's a tough place to live in the wintertime, the windows were all icy, whew!), I climbed under my three comforters and waited a bit. The old folks would go to bed early, then I went down to the den and was dialing this Philco radio and found the Grand Old Opry station and Ernest Tubb. I loved that song I heard, and that man's rich baritone voice. Maybe me being an orphan moved me or something, but anyhow, I got into this song, this love song he sang, and that's what I write today."

I had Harlan photocopy a lot of his sheet music for me in his basement, so I could tape it to his body and have it appear to flow out from him. I found two little songbirds in cages in the kitchen and placed them in the foreground on the sheet music, and then I took some shots without them. When I later had prints blown up from the proofs, I found the birds were too much for they took away from the character of this man's face.

I particularly enjoyed the whimsicality of so many of the country musicians I met, and the very characters they created out of themselves—Boxcar Willie with his train whistle call; Pee Wee King, co-author of "Tennessee Waltz," who played his accordion for me in the old, angel-filled cemetery where I photographed him; John Hartford, the riverboat singer who kept doing a little shuffling dance while we tried to adhere small riverboats to his pant leg, so we could have them seem to come up out of the river onto his leg. Sometimes he would throw back his head and laugh heartily to the sky, a laugh for himself, not to be shared, just to be laughing. He later told me that the riverboats made him think of spiders coming up out of the water.

Hugh Howell, a bus driver, spends seven months of the year on the road, from March 'til September, doing fifteen to sixteen shows a month, with "one day of travel between shows." (The rest of the year he is an auctioneer of farm equipment and raises breed cattle on his third generation farm east of Nashville, on river-bottom land along Neely's Bend.) He became interested in country music in the second grade, he said, when he became friends with Gary Scruggs, son of the greatest living banjo player Earl Scruggs. Hugh would spend the night at Gary's house. "Earl was a very quiet man with a dry humor; he would make us laugh by reading the phone book to us." When Earl wasn't traveling he would help Gary and Hugh play the guitar with him. "He would tell us, if you're going to play, play correct."

One of the reasons why I wanted to photograph a country music bus driver was because I wanted to know what the world is like in there, and where they go and what they see, and what Hugh's life is like up there in front of the bus.

"The country music bus is a land yacht," Hugh told me. "It takes the show to the people. It can sleep nine to twelve people, depending on the bus. It's a motor home with sleeping quarters. There are bunks, like berths on a train, compartments that stack three high. And there's usually two lounge areas, TV sets, VCRs, recording equipment, and a small gallery for a microwave oven, a refrigerator for snacks.

"Then there are the musicians' particular instruments. The musician has such a personal relationship with his instrument that he keeps it with him. So we have the fiddles, and guitars, whatever. The amplifiers, PA equipment, lights go by truck. Most of the travel is at night when everyone sleeps or watches movies. The performance is the exercise, when the performance is over we get back on the bus and head on out. We cover forty states, from the upper peninsula of Canada, right on down through Texas to the Mexican border—one end of the map to the other. I've been to all the continental United States and have crossed five provinces of Canada."

Waylon Jennings and Porter Wagoner told me moving stories about early times in their lives, stories that suggested ideas for photographs. Waylon said, "I grew up in West Texas, about a hundred miles directly south of Amarillo, in a place called Littlefields. My dad, William Albert, was a farm laborer. He would farm and plow and work from sunup to sundown, and then milk some twenty-odd head of cattle. He earned one dollar a day. My momma, Loreen Beatrice, had to take us sometimes to neighbors to get something to eat. We would walk. The land was flat. You could see as far as you wanted to in West Texas (and didn't want to!). The wind would be blowing. It blew almost all the time. It would break through the siding on the wood houses, so they were patched up with tar paper. You see, the wind would blow at times as high as seventy to eighty miles an hour, and we would have sandstorms that would boil up. You could see them coming, all of the boiling of dust and that would go on for three or four day, day and night. At that time there was nothing between us and New Mexico, and no matter what kind of windows you had, there would be a big bunch of sand right under the windowsill in any house. The dust got all over you, even in your mouth. I can remember grabbing hold of a light post to hang on. Sometimes it got completely dark and the chickens would roost at twelve noon. I can hear the moaning sound forever in my life.

"Well, I came from this to Nashville, and there was this system, this way of doing things. It was like assembly-line music. You would go in and take four songs, and then do them in three hours no matter what happened. You would use their musicians, and they had the producers. You had to use their producers and their studios. One time I had a producer and I came back a week later, and I couldn't recognize my song because he had put this and that in it. For me a record is like a picture, and you should be able to see it, and when you get through, it should look like that. It was so frustrating, you had no control.

"And they wanted you to dress a certain way—clean-cut looking—and they didn't want the long hair, and there was this big rhinestone thing. I swear everyone wore rhinestones on their shorts. This was round the mid-sixties, and I was like someone from outer space because I wore Levis, and I didn't want to wear rhinestones, and I wanted to use my own group when I recorded, and I wanted to pick my own songs. For them, this was unbelievable. Finally, I saw that I couldn't do what they were wanting me to do. You know, you go in and let them play the music and you just sing. And I couldn't do that because I had rhythms in my mind and I had leads in my mind, and they just weren't ready for that. I just had to balk and stop and say, 'I'm not going to do it that way any more,' and so I went over to another studio and finally got a production deal, but I was still stuck in their studios, so I just went to another studio and recorded an album. I have a friend, Willie Nelson, and I said 'Come help me with this,' and so we went over there and had a wonderful time recording. That's what music is about, and that's what I wanted to do. I didn't care how much it cost to record an album, whatever it cost to make it wonderful, and to make you proud of it. When it comes out of there they should say, 'that is Waylon.' That album was called, 'The Outlaw,' with Waylon and Willie, and my wife Jessi, and Tom Paul. It was the first million-selling album in country music, certified, and I produced it, and everything."

Waylon Jennings, "The Outlaw," hanging onto a lamp post in a west Texas dust storm—single-mindedly, surviving, holding on to his existence with his own two hands. Perhaps he carried that single-mindedness with him to Nashville to "work outside of a working system:" that is what outlaw means, he told me. So I photographed him with his back to the camera, turning away from the system, with his trademark guitar slung over his shoulder; to the right of him an old abandoned hay cutter, with teeth still sharp, a strong cutting edge; in front of him a fence with no wires, no boards, just free open poles. On his left, mist rose from a heavy summer rainstorm from the hills.

Porter Wagoner's story was quite different. "I wasn't really trying to get in the music business. I was discovered singing in a little grocery store, in West Plains, Missouri, that's my hometown. The man that ran the store liked to hear me sing, so he told me to bring my guitar and put it in the back of the store and when we would have time, when there wasn't anything much going on in the store, he'd ask me to get my guitar and sing three or four songs. Then he got the idea to put me on the radio. We had a radio station there—KWPM—and he talked to them about doing a remote three days a week from his store, setting up a microphone there and a line into the radio station, where every morning I would go down and open up the store at five-thirty in the morning and I would go on the air for fifteen minutes. I would sing a few songs to advertise our specials in the store for the day. Well, when we did that the business just quadrupled. Then one morning I went in to do the radio show and there was this big black Lincoln settin' out in front of the store. Well, I had become so popular, I thought it was maybe Al Capone or one of the gangsters coming to assassinate me. It really made me very nervous, because I didn't know who it was or anything, one guy sitting in the car by himself, in a big black Lincoln. Anyway, I went in and it got time for me to go on the air, and as soon as I got off the guy got out and came in the store. He introduced himself and said, 'I'm Lou Black from Springfield and KWPO.' He told me how he heard about me and so forth, and said, 'I wanted to see if you'd be interested in coming to Springfield and being on our radio station there, KWPO.' So naturally I said yeah. That's kinda how I began in the business. I didn't do it for the money. I wasn't planning on it. I was working in a grocery store when it kinda discovered me."

Porter Wagoner is one of the most colorful Grand Old Opry members. He wears rhinestone suits, invented by Mr. Nudie in California. "It was his idea to do the rhinestones cause nobody had wore them up until that time; there had been no outfits made with rhinestones on them before 1953. He had made clothes for movie stars like Gene Autry and Roy Rogers and Tom Mix, and some of those people, but then he got the idea of the glitter, and in fact he told me when he made this first suit for me—he said, 'I'm gonna make you a suit that when you come on stage people will go wow, look at that, wow.' I had no idea what he was talking about, but that's what he had in mind then. Because the first time I put the suit on was in 1953 and I sang a song called 'Company's Comin'' that I had just recorded, and I came on the stage of the Jewel Theater in Springfield, Missouri. Well, people had never seen a rhinestone outfit. When I walked out on stage, I mean they said *wow*, there was an excitement there that had never happened before in my career. That's back before Liberace or Elvis or any of them people. When I got my first suit I put it on and took it off, my sister told me, eleven times. I'd sit around and forty-five minutes later I'd be getting the suit out again. I couldn't wait to see it again, on me. It was a peach-colored outfit that was just tremendous. It had rhinestone covered wagons. There was a beautiful covered wagon on the back of it with rhinestones all over it, and God it was just breathtaking to me. And on the legs of it he [Mr. Nudie] had made like a stage coach with horses in front of it, and a guy sitting on the stage coach with a whip, and the whip was done in rhinestones and stuff. It was beautiful and it was artistic too. Manuel, who used to work for Mr. Nudie, is making my clothes now. He's a brilliant man. He did all the early Clint Eastwood movies, and Dirty Harry, and he was the one who designed the jumpsuit for Elvis that he wore all the time on his big things in Las Vegas."

Porter Wagoner was placed before a Nashville monument called The Parthenon, as he is a monument in the country music business, and he was dressed in a rhinestone suit by Manuel. I tried to make Porter Wagoner look noble, for there is a nobility to these country music singers.

Light is important to me and I looked for it always on my walks in Mr. Ragsdale's field. I went about, here and there, and suddenly I saw it, the *light*. It didn't happen very often. It was rare.

How can I tell you what the light said; it is so hard to do it in words. It speaks back so. You become terribly excited as an artist, and you cry out within yourself, "there it is, the light, I must get it!"

One afternoon, about three-thirty, I was in a thinking mood. I walked across the field thinking, looking down, and thinking, and when I got to the end of the field, I looked up to my left, to the hills, and there it was, a kind of light that spoke magic. It was very gentle, very fine, soft, and golden. The sun was low over the hills, at an angle, and it seemed to infuse the leaves of the trees at the top of the hill with a kind of magical energy that spoke a promise of things finer and purer—things kinder. It invited one to come into that magical moment and be taken away to a better place. It was so gently beautiful, you forgot about yourself, for the moment, as you went *there*, to it. "There it is!" I thought to myself, "This is such a special light, I'm sure it only comes at this time of year." I began to be anxious about an appropriate connection, a singer to photograph in this light. Then it came to me. I had seen recently a Grand Ole Opry member, Skeeter Davis, sing on TNN television at the Opry. Curiously, she lived just a few miles away from Mr. Ragsdale's field. I had noticed that Skeeter had had wonderful hair, long, wavy and blond—spiritual hair. She looked like one of the subjects in a small intimate fifteenth-century Italian religious painting, like a Fra Angelico. She was perfect.

Eagles Creek ran behind the log cabin where Skeeter Davis was born, in northern Kentucky, Dry Ridge, in 1931. Her father grew corn and tobacco and "of course my mother never worked, she was always havin' babies. There were seven of us, Buddy Shirley, Shirley Catherine, Harold Lee, Merrill Dean, Caroline Sue, and Leona Anne, three brothers and three sisters.

"I was always missin'. I was always goin' here or goin' there, from a very early age. I'd be in the creek or goin' to the neighbors—and then they'd find me. So grandpoppy said that I was like a skeeter—you'd see it, and then it's gone.

"I liked to go up to my hill, I called it, 'Holy Hill,' and I'd go up there and any animal that wasn't confined by the pen would follow me up, the goats, the horses, the cows, the chickens, the pigs. My mother would look up and say, 'well, there goes St. Francis.' One day, on top of the hill, I was crying over the loss of a horse we had to put to sleep, and I looked up and the animals weren't just standing out there, they had surrounded me, and were looking at me, sort of comforting like. It was kind of special.

"On Tuesday nights my father ran the little theater in Dry Ridge. It was the only theater for miles and miles and miles around. So he would take turns letting us go. So I would see the movie stars, Betty Hutton and Betty Grable and June Haver.

"The next day after the movie I would get all the big empty gallon molasses buckets and set them in a row upside down as stools for my brothers and sisters. Then I would get the shears from the barn and cut out strips from old coffee tins, just so wide. Then I would put paper from the catalog round the strips and roll my hair and try to do it in a pageboy. When I took those out, I'd always have two kinks where the tin folded down. Then I would sit my brothers and sisters on the buckets and I would be Betty Grable. I would mimic her, and sing. I sang 'My Rocky Horse Ran Away,' and I did cartwheels. The wildest thing to me is that they paid attention, it actually kept them all there. You know what's amazing, nobody else around was doing that. I don't know how I thought to do it, but they all thought I was something."

I wish I could have gone on to cover every room of the country music scene, to have shared some time will all of the great legends of country music, and the wonderful young up and coming singers, so full of hope and expectancy. But that was not to be, for many country music singers do not live in Nashville where I was based. Willie Nelson and George Strait are in Texas, Merle Haggard and Dwight Yoakam are in California, and others, at least according to their managers, have such a profound dislike of being photographed, that they insist that the experience be kept to an absolute minimum. When passing briefly through Nashville for a recording session in a heavily jammed schedule the thought of having to pose for a photograph on top of everything else would be for them, the managers indicated, like having to take a bath with a skunk.

But as for me, I hope the viewer's experience will be like mine—seeing this most original world like a magic box with many unexpected rooms—and be taken away for a moment or two into its magic.

I want to thank so much those who gave time from their busy lives to pose for me, so that we could all work together to say something about this special American art form, country music. The artist simply cannot do it all alone. So many helped, I cannot name them all, but I hope everyone will know how grateful I am. Jessi Colter, was a kind help when I began my project, and I appreciate the help with ideas that Jeannie Seeley, Mr. and Mrs. William Weaver

III, Alanna Nash, and Sandra and Dick Fulton gave; also Bonnie Rasmussen Taggert, Chet Atkins, Bill Ivey, Jo Walker Meador, and Frances Preston. I also thank the women of Belle Meade, whose energy and strong encouragement helped to carry me through: Martha Ingram, Jackie Thompson, Alice Mathews, Kathy Menefee, Barbara Chazen, Jane Eskind, Betsy Lindseth, and Ellen Duncan, for her help when I first came to Nashville. Lois Riggins-Ezell, Director of the Tennessee State Museum showed some great courage in her belief early on in the project and Leigh R. Hendry, Director of Special Projects at the museum worked beyond the call of duty. I want to thank Vanessa Ware and Claudia McConnell and Rosemay Wade for their photo-styling; Rique and Earl of Trumps for their hairstyling; Janice Pyle, Barry Jones, Leigh Bradford, and LaLah Humble for their photo assistance. Judy Silvia, Birgette and Lou Hilton, Clover Nicholas, and Faye Scheuch, gave fine encouragement early in my career and education, and later on, Holly Solomon and Frank Fowler. Thanks to the von Matthiessen family, Mr. and Mrs. James Lanney, Priscilla Janney-Pace, Cracker Barrel Old Country Store, Inc., and Dan Evins and O. E. Philpot at Cracker Barrel for the support of the project. Agfa supplied a generous amount of printing paper, Portriga and Insignia, with which I make my vision—this paper speaks for me. I made the image of Boxcar Willie with the loan of some equipment from Leica. Hasselblad donated the camera I used to create the image of Mae Axton. Performance Costume Rental, Liberty Party, White Oak Taxidermy, the Cumberland Museum, provided necessary props. The wonderful southern writer-artist Eugene Walter in Mobile, Alabama, did the collages of Ray Stevens and Roger Miller and Connie Smith. Janet E. Williams supplied the biographies, and the photographs used in the Alan Mayor image were by photographer Frank Ockenfels III. Very importantly, I want to thank my printer, Edwin Acevedo, for all these years of working with me and helping to create the look I need, and to the Lexington lab for filling in on emergency quick-rush loose ends. Finally, I appreciate the sensitive effort to understand my vision, and the push for excellence of my editor, Wendy Batteau, and the patient persistence of her assistant, Patrick Groom, to make sure that all the necessary parts of the book were brought together on time. And I also thank my literary agent, Tim Seldes, and his assistant, Joseph Regal, for their encouragement.

—MARIA VON MATTHIESSEN

Songs from the Hills

"Whispering" Bill Anderson

Boxcar Willie

Kitty Wells

4

Jeannie Seeley

Roy Acuff 5

Earl Scruggs

Bill Monroe

Little Jimmy Dickens

Chet Atkins

Jack Greene

June Carter Cash

Owen Bradley

Hank Snow

Pee Wee King

Eddy Arnold

Loretta Lynn's hands

Loretta Lynn

Jimmy C. Newman and Cajun Country

Wilma Lee Cooper

Tom T. Hall

Johnny Russell

22

Porter Wagoner

24

Skeeter Davis

Jerry Reed

Brentwood, Tennessee

Kingston Springs, Tennessee

Jeannie C. Riley

Ray Stevens

Ronnie Milsap

Charley Pride

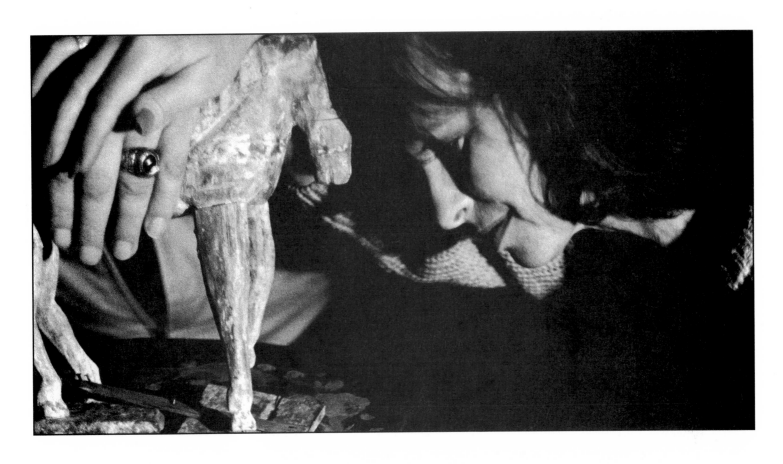

Jessi Colter and Waylon Jennings' hand

Billy Joe Royal

Janie Frickie

36

Larry Gatlin

Emmylou Harris

Connie Smith

Bobby Bare

Razzy Bailey

William Lee Golden

T. G. Sheppard

Marty Stuart (right) *with Manuel* (left)

The Forester Sisters

Stella Parton

45

Del Reeves

Jeanne Pruett

Hank Thompson

48

Don Williams

Ronnie McDowell with sons

Stonewall Jackson

John Hartford

Roger Miller

Kingston Springs, Tennessee

Kingston Springs, Tennessee

55

David Schnaufer

Marty Lanham

Buddy Emmons

Mark O'Connor

Clinton Gregory

Charlie McCoy

Harlan Howard

Mae Axton

Paul Overstreet with family

Dean Dillon

Linda Davis

Jerry Douglas

67

Victoria Shaw

Stephanie Davis

Marshall Chapman

Kevin Welch

Vanessa Ware

Diana Christian with Rique

The Johnson Sisters

Hugh Howell

Brentwood, Tennessee

Brentwood, Tennessee

Graceland

Dan Seals

Holly Dunn   *Opposite: Charlie Daniels*

Mike Reid

Rosanne Cash

84

T. Graham Brown and son

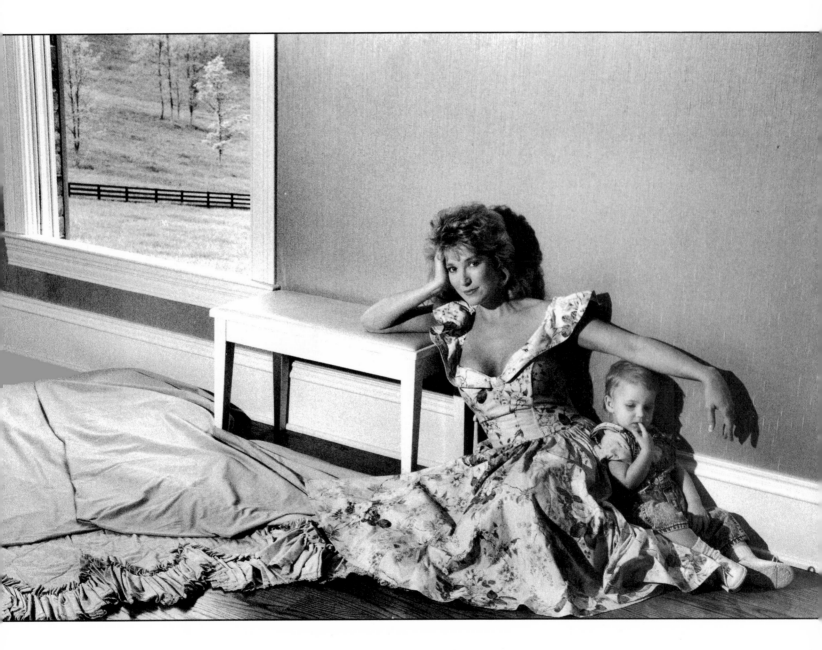

Tanya Tucker and daughter

Paulette Carlson

The Bellamy Brothers

88 *B.J. Thomas   Opposite: Rodney Crowell*

Joe Diffie with Earl Pack

Hal Ketchum

Jann Browne

Lionel Cartwright

93

Kelly Willis

Bill Miller

Shawn Camp

Stacy Dean Campbell with Alan Mayor

Radney Foster

Mark Collie

Wild Rose

Riders in the Sky

Dixiana

Diamond Rio

Trisha Yearwood

Michelle Wright

106   *Maura O'Connell*

Mark Chesnutt

Billy Ray Cyrus

Suzy Bogguss

Sawyer Brown

Kathy Mattea with Jon Vezner

111

Alison Krauss

Brooks & Dunn

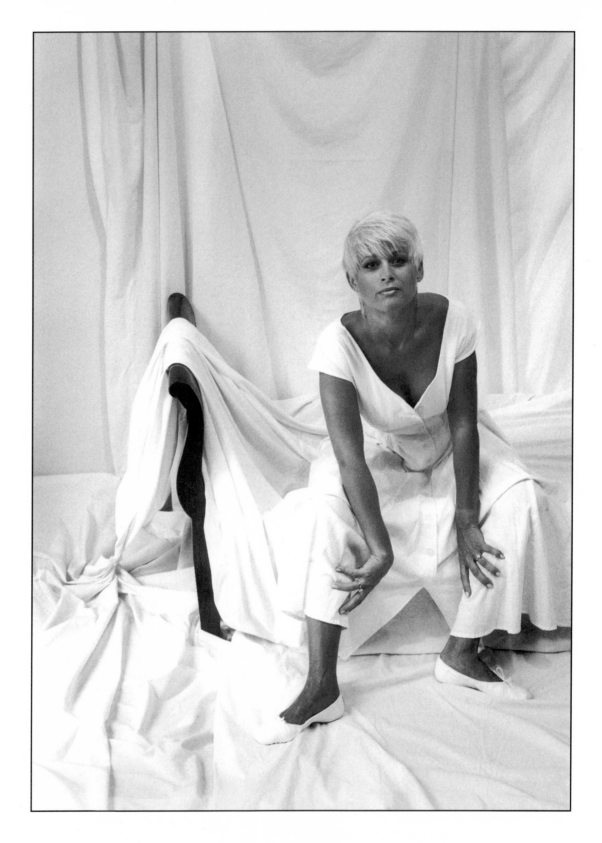

Lorrie Morgan

Vince Gill

Tennesee Grass

Minnie Pearl's hat

BIOGRAPHIES

Only a life-threatening case of sunstroke kept ROY ACUFF from a professional baseball career. During his convalescence, he decided to embark on an entertainment career. Debuting on the Grand Ole Opry in 1938, he went on to earn the nickname "King of Country Music" and was elected to the Country Music Hall of Fame in 1962. Acuff, whose career spanned seven decades, died in 1992.

BILL ANDERSON first found success as a songwriter when his tune "City Lights" became a hit for Ray Price. As a singer, his recordings of "Tip of my Fingers" and "Po' Folks" are regarded as country classics. The South Carolina native is one of the most popular members of the Grand Ole Opry.

EDDY ARNOLD was country music's first crossover artist, finding worldwide fame with hits like "Make the World Go Away," "Bouquet of Roses," and "Then You Can Tell Me Goodbye." Elected to the Country Music Hall of Fame in 1966, Arnold hosted his own television show and continues to be one of country music's most enduring and popular entertainers.

CHET ATKINS is the idol of legions of guitarists, including Vince Gill, Mark Knopfler of the rock group Dire Straits, and jazz musician Earl Klugh. A native of Tennessee and a member of the Country Music Hall of Fame, he proudly signs his name "Chet Atkins, C.G.P." (certified guitar player).

MAE AXTON wrote one of Elvis Presley's biggest hits, "Heartbreak Hotel," establishing herself as one of the most famous songwriters in the music industry. She is also the mother of entertainer Hoyt Axton, who proved he inherited his mother's genius by writing songs including "Joy to the World" for Three Dog Night.

After twenty years of struggle, frustration, and failure, RAZZY BAILEY finally found country stardom with "What Time Do You Have to Be Back in Heaven?" in 1978. Other hits for the Alabama native include "Midnight Hauler" and "She Left Love All Over Me."

Armed with an independent spirit and an innovative nature, BOBBY BARE pushed the boundaries of traditional country music in the 1960s. One of Music City's most renowned songwriters, he was also a successful recording artist with hits including "Detroit City" and "500 Miles Away From Home."

Hailing from Florida, Howard and David Bellamy—the BELLAMY BROTHERS—remain one of country music's most popular duos. The brothers first found fame with the huge country-rock hit "Let Your Love Flow." Their 1979 song "If I Said You Had a Beautiful Body (Would You Hold It Against Me?)" was the most successful country song of the year in England, where it reached the number-three position on the pop chart.

After earning a degree in metalsmithery, SUZY BOGGUSS toured the country on the club circuit before heading to Nashville in search of a record deal. Hits like "Aces," "Letting Go," and "Someday Soon" brought her the Country Music Association's prestigious Horizon Award in 1992.

Producer OWEN BRADLEY is one of the creators of the famed "Nashville sound" of the 1950s and 1960s. His work with Ernest Tubb, Red Foley, Patsy Cline, Brenda Lee, Loretta Lynn, Webb Pierce, and many other top country stars assured him a place in the Country Music Hall of Fame, to which he was elected in 1974.

Kix BROOKS & Ronnie DUNN were paired as a songwriting team by Arista Records head Tim DuBois in 1990. Two years later, they were named Vocal Duo of the Year by the Country Music Association and have a string of number-one hits, including "Brand New Man," "Boot Scootin' Boogie," and "Neon Moon."

T. GRAHAM BROWN launched his music career while attending the University of Georgia. Adding soulful blues and rock to contemporary country music, he has created a distinctive vocal style that is unrivaled. Hits include "Darlene," "Tell It Like It Used to Be," and "Don't Go Out," a duet with Tanya Tucker.

Indiana native JANN BROWNE spent two years with country swing band Asleep at the Wheel before embarking on a solo career in 1983. Also a successful songwriter, her hits include "Tell Me Why" and "You Ain't Down Home."

SHAWN CAMP promises to be one of country music's most noteworthy new artists. The Arkansas native has performed with The Osborne Brothers, Suzy Bogguss, Alan Jackson, Trisha Yearwood, and others. He was recently signed by Warner Bros. Records.

STACY DEAN CAMPBELL was about to join the Oklahoma County Sheriff's Department as a deputy when stardom beckoned. He is one of country music's rising stars, with songs like "Rosalie" and "Poor Man's Rose."

After leading the country band Highway 101 to critical acclaim with hits like "The Bed He Made for Me," PAULETTE CARLSON left the group to pursue a solo career in 1991. She has also written songs that have been recorded by Gail Davies and Tammy Wynette.

LIONEL CARTWRIGHT hit Music City with a vengeance in the mid-1980s, finding success with songs such as "Give Me His Last Chance" and "I Watched It All on My Radio." He got his start in Nashville as a featured performer, arranger, and musical director for *I-40 Paradise,* a series on TNN: The Nashville Network.

JUNE CARTER CASH is one of the most revered talents in country music. A daughter of the legendary Mother Maybelle Carter, she toured with her sisters Anita and Helen before going solo. Married to Johnny Cash just one week after they won a Grammy award for their recording of "Jackson," she co-wrote one of his biggest hits, "Ring of Fire."

ROSANNE CASH continues the musical family tradition of her father, Johnny Cash. After scoring with country hits such as "Seven Year Ache," "Tennessee Flat Top Box," and "I Don't Know Why You Don't Want Me," the Grammy-winning singer/songwriter set her eyes on pop stardom and moved to New York in 1992.

MARSHALL CHAPMAN is one of Nashville's most popular club singers. She is frequently found performing to standing-room-only crowds at the famed Bluebird Cafe and other nightspots with her band, The Love Slaves.

MARK CHESNUTT was a local star in his hometown of Beaumont, Texas, where he played for standing-room-only crowds at Cutter's. He has become one of the most successful new country stars of the 1990s, with hits like "Brother Jukebox" and "Too Cold at Home."

DIANA CHRISTIAN is a Nashville background singer, providing harmonies for many of country music's most popular entertainers. She has performed with numerous singers, including the legendary Bill Monroe.

MARK COLLIE's exotic looks and distinctive voice have made him a favorite on the club circuit in western Tennessee for several years. Country fans nationwide are quickly joining the throng as they tune in to hits like "Only the Man in the Moon Is Crying" and "She's Never Comin' Back." The gifted singer/songwriter lives in Nashville with his wife Anne, son Nathan, and dog (a collie, of course) Amos.

WILMA LEE COOPER, together with her late husband Stoney, was a regular on the WWVA Wheeling Jamboree form 1947 until they became members of the Grand Ole Opry in 1957. Wilma Lee continues to be a favorite of Opry audiences.

RODNEY CROWELL stepped into music history when five singles from his 1988 album *Diamonds and Dirt* went to number one. The Grammy-winning singer/songwriter, a native of Texas, was once a member of Emmylou Harris's Hot Band. His hits include "Till I Gain Control Again," "Above and Beyond," and "After All This Time."

BILLY RAY CYRUS was country music's biggest success story of 1992. His single, "Achy Breaky Heart," became an international phenomenon and resulted in a television special for the Kentucky native. Critics were silenced when his second single, "Could've Been Me," also topped the charts.

CHARLIE DANIELS brought southern rock into country music with songs like "The South's Gonna Do It Again," "The Devil Went Down to Georgia," for which he won a 1979 Grammy Award, and "In America." The South Carolina native is also renowned for his acts of humanitarianism, which include his annual Volunteer Jam.

LINDA DAVIS made her singing debut on the East Texas Gary Jamboree at the age of six. Since then, she has become one of Nashville's most versatile singers. In addition to solo success, she has toured with Reba McEntire and others.

SKEETER DAVIS, born Mary Frances Penick, was on the road to fame as one-half of the Davis Sisters when she was critically injured and partner Betty Jack Davis was killed in a car accident. Following a lengthy convalescence, she went on to find success as a solo artist with hits such as "The End of the World" and "Gonna Get Along Without You Now." She has been a member of the Grand Ole Opry since 1959.

STEPHANIE DAVIS is one of country music's most promising new talents. Already known as a top-notch songwriter, she was recently signed by Asylum Records.

The members of DIAMOND RIO—Marty Roe, Jimmy Olander, Dana Williams, Gene Johnson, Dan Truman, and Brian Prout—cite a diversity of influences, ranging from legendary bluegrass duo the Osborne Brothers to the Beatles. The band was originally called the Tennessee River Boys.

LITTLE JIMMY DICKENS began his professional career in 1942 as Jimmy the Kid. A member of the Grand Ole Opry since 1948, his numerous hits include "Country Boy," "I'm Little but I'm Loud," and "May the Bird of Paradise Fly Up Your Nose."

When he lost his job at a foundry in Velma, Oklahoma, JOE DIFFIE packed his bags and moved to Nashville in 1986. His work as a demo singer caught the attention of Epic Records, and soon Diffie was on the charts with hits like "New Way to Light Up an Old Flame" and "If the Devil Danced in Empty Pockets."

DEAN DILLON, a native of Lake City, Tennessee, is the talent responsible for many of George Strait's biggest hits, including "The Chair," "Marina Del Ray," "Nobody in His Right Mind Would Have Left Her," and "Ocean Front Property." He once performed at Opryland USA theme park and has also released several albums of his own.

The members of DIXIANA—Cindy Murphey, Mark Lister, Phil Lister, Randall Griffith, and Colonel Shuford—came together in 1986, becoming a popular regional band in the area of Greenville, South Carolina. Nashville beckoned in 1991, and they found a national audience with "Waiting for the Deal to Go Down."

JERRY DOUGLAS can be described in one word: superpicker. A virtuoso on the Dobro, he also plays mandolin and guitar. The Ohio native is one of Nashville's busiest session players and has also released several albums of his own.

HOLLY DUNN jumped into the country music spotlight in 1987 with "Daddy's Hands," a song she wrote as a Father's Day gift to her dad. A Country Music Association Award winner, her other hits include "Are You Gonna Love Me" and "Love Someone Like Me."

BUDDY EMMONS has been one of Nashville's most accomplished musicians for over twenty years. A specialist on the steel guitar, he also plays piano and bass. In addition to doing extensive session work, he has toured with Ernest Tubb, Roger Miller, Ray Price, and Linda Ronstadt.

THE FORESTER SISTERS—June, Kim, Kathy, and Christy—hail from Lookout Mountain, Georgia. After fine-tuning their vocal harmonies at church, they found mainstream success in country music with songs like "I Fell in Love Again Last Night" and "Mama's Never Seen Those Eyes."

RADNEY FOSTER was one-half of Foster & Lloyd, a country duo that had fans taking notice in the late 1980s. Now concentrating on his solo career, the Texas singer/songwriter is quickly restaking a claim on the charts with tunes including "Nobody Wins" and "Just Call Me Lonesome."

JANIE FRICKIE is not only one of country music's most popular singers, she's also the voice heard on national commercials for 7-Up, Pizza Hut, United Airlines, and many others. A former Country Music Association Female Vocalist of the Year, her hits include "Come a little Bit Closer" and "Baby It's You."

LARRY GATLIN was discovered by country superstar Dottie West in the early 1970s. Spurred by her encouragement, he found success (along with brothers Steve and Rudy) with hits like "Houston," "Broken Lady," and "All the Gold in California." He made his Broadway debut in 1993 starring in *The Will Rogers Follies.*

VINCE GILL is one of the most accomplished guitarists in country music today. A former member of the pop band Pure Prairie League, his sterling vocals have made him a country superstar. The Grammy-winning artist is also a multiple Country Music Association award winner. He is married to Janis Gill, one-half of the Sweethearts of the Rodeo.

WILLIAM LEE GOLDEN had been a member of the Oak Ridge Boys for over thirty years when he left the group to pursue a solo career. A native of Alabama, he lives in a converted slave cabin on his Hendersonville, Tennessee, estate. Golden's sons Rusty and Chris are also country singers.

GRACELAND, located in Memphis, Tennessee, was the home of Elvis Presley.

JACK GREENE's career began when he toured as a member of Ernest Tubb's band. "The Last Letter" launched his solo career, and he was the first recipient of the Country Music Association's Male Vocalist of the Year Award in 1967.

CLINTON GREGORY is a fifth-generation fiddle player who picked up his instrument at the age of three. A former member of Suzy Bogguss's road band, he hit the big time with "(If It Weren't for Country Music) I'd Go Crazy" in 1991.

TOM T. HALL is known as the "Storyteller," and for good reason. His story songs, including "HarperValley PTA," have become country classics. His own singing career flourished with hits like "Old Dogs, Children and Watermelon Wine," "The Year That Clayton Delaney Died," and "I Love."

EMMYLOU HARRIS brings style and elegance to country music. Her crystal-clear vocals on songs like "Together Again" and "Two More Bottles of Wine" have made her one of country music's most popular singers. The Grammy-winning Alabama native is a member of the Grand Ole Opry.

JOHN HARTFORD's "Gentle On My Mind" has become one of the most popular country songs ever written. A part-time riverboat captain, Hartford basked in the spotlight as a featured performer on the *Glen Campbell Hour* television series in 1969. A multiple Grammy winner, Hartford continues to perform folk-country music with a bluegrass flavor.

HARLAN HOWARD is often referred to as the king of country songwriters. A member of the

Nashville Songwriters Association International Hall of Fame, he has written some of country music's most famous classic tunes, including "Heartaches by the Number," "I've Got a Tiger by the Tail," and "I Fall to Pieces."

HUGH HOWELL has been an entertainment tour bus driver for twenty years. The Nashville native has driven everyone from Earl Scruggs to USWA wrestlers to Clinton Gregory.

Following his discharge from the Navy in 1954, STONEWALL JACKSON (yes that's his real name) journeyed to Nashville to pursue a career. The move paid off when songs like "Waterloo" and "Life to Go" brought him national acclaim.

WAYLON JENNINGS is a country music legend. One of the leaders of the "outlaw movement" during the mid-1970s, Jennings has recorded numerous hits including "Luckenbach, Texas," "Good Hearted Woman" with Willie Nelson, and "Can't You See." His wife, JESSI COLTER, gained national acclaim with "I'm Not Lisa" in 1975. Her first marriage to rock 'n' roll guitarist Duane Eddy lasted eight years. Following her marriage to Jennings, she put her career on the back burner to concentrate on her husband and child.

When sisters LORETTA, LOUDILLA, and KAY JOHNSON started a fan club for Loretta Lynn, they had no idea it would lead to the formation of the International Fan Club Organization in 1965. Under their supervision, IFCO has become the guiding organization for all country music fan clubs and has more than 350 member fan clubs.

HAL KETCHUM took the long road to Nashville. From his hometown in upstate New York, he moved to Austin, Texas, before heading to Music City USA. His recording of "Small Town Saturday Night" was one of the most-played songs of 1991.

Not only is PEE WEE KING one of country music's most beloved singers and bandleaders, he is also a renowned songwriter, having co-written the country classic "Tennessee Waltz." The Wisconsin native was elected to the Country Music Hall of Fame in 1974.

ALISON KRAUSS is one of bluegrass music's biggest new stars. A multiple Grammy Award winner, she recorded her first album at the age of fifteen and jumped into the spotlight with "I've Got That Old Feeling" in 1991.

MARTY LANHAM earned a reputation as the foremost restorer of vintage musical instruments in the world for the past twenty-six years. He also handcrafts guitars and banjos, each of which takes over four months to construct. The California native has restored Hank Williams's Martin D45 guitar, which currently belongs to Marty Stuart, and a guitar of the legendary Jimmie Rodgers, which is now in the Country Music Hall of Fame, among others.

LORETTA LYNN is one of country music's first female superstars. Her autobiography, *Coal Miner's Daughter*, was turned into an Academy Award–winning motion picture in 1980. In addition to an overwhelming solo career, she was part of one of country music's most successful duos, with Conway Twitty. Lynn was elected to the Country Music Hall of Fame in 1988.

CHARLIE MCCOY has been one of country music's most popular musicians—specializing on the harmonica—for years. In addition to releasing several solo albums, he has played on sessions for numerous entertainers, including Bob Dylan, Joan Baez, and Ringo Starr.

RONNIE MCDOWELL became a fixture on the country charts with "The King Is Gone," a tribute to Elvis Presley, in 1977. Since then, his talents as a singer and songwriter have been recognized by fans nationwide.

MANUEL was a protégé of famed Hollywood clothier Nudie Cohen. Since striking out on his own, he has established himself as *the* designer for country music's stars. His list of clients includes Marty Stuart, Dwight Yoakam, Emmylou Harris, and Wynonna Judd, to name a few.

KATHY MATTEA's sterling vocals were temporarily silenced in 1992 following vocal cord surgery. A former CMA Female Vocalist of the Year, she is married to songwriter JON VEZNER, who co-wrote her award-winning hit, "Where've You Been?"

ALAN MAYOR is one of the few people who attends virtually every major country music event, from album parties to award shows. One of Nashville's busiest photographers, he has captured the spirit of all of today's country entertainers on film.

Native American BILL MILLER combines his contemporary acoustic music with story-oriented, slice-of-life gems to create a fresh, original sound that celebrates the triumph of the human spirit. He grew up on an Indian reservation in central Wisconsin and studied art at the University of Wisconsin-LaCrosse on a scholarship.

ROGER MILLER was one of the music industry's greatest wits. He won eleven Grammy awards in two years, with songs like "King of the Road" and "Dang Me." Raised in Erick, Oklahoma, he also composed the Tony Award–winning score of Broadway's "Big River." One of the most celebrated songwriters of the twentieth century, Miller died in 1992.

By the end of the 1970s, RONNIE MILSAP had been honored with practically every country music award for which he was eligible. His string of hits includes "Stranger in My House," "There's No Getting Over Me," "Legend in My Time," and "Lost in the Fifties Tonight."

The "father of bluegrass music," BILL MONROE is one of the few individuals who can be credited with the creation of a new type of music. He is still a regular on the Grand Ole Opry, which he joined in 1939, and was elected to the Country Music Hall of Fame in 1970.

LORRIE MORGAN proudly carries on the legacy of her father, the legendary George Morgan. She first performed on the Grand Ole Opry at the age of twelve, and after finding commercial success in the 1990s became a member of the prestigious venue.

JIMMY C. NEWMAN grew up in the bayou country of Louisiana and developed his own musical style, mixing traditional Cajun sounds with country music. A member of the Grand Ole Opry since 1956, he and his Cajun Country band are frequent visitors to Europe, where they enjoy considerable popularity.

Irish songstress MAURA O'CONNELL is known as a gifted interpreter. Her full-throated vocals showcase her refreshing brand of folk music with warmth, tenderness, and power.

Multi-instrumentalist MARK O'CONNOR has been referred to as "the greatest musician on the planet" by Vince Gill. Already an accomplished musician on guitar, mandolin, banjo, steel guitar, and Dobro, he taught himself to play the fiddle at the age of eleven and won every major fiddle contest in the country by the time he was a senior in high school. He is universally acclaimed as a pure musical genius by his peers.

The songs of PAUL OVERSTREET reflect his commitments to God, family, and the values of common people. He first found success as a songwriter with hits like "Forever and Ever, Amen" and "On the Other Hand" and is now one of country music's most popular singers. Hits like "All the Fun," "Seein' My Father in Me," and "Sowin' Love" are affirmations of his positive beliefs.

EARL PACK is a farmer from White Station, Tennessee.

STELLA PARTON is proof that musical ability runs in families. Following in her older sister Dolly's footsteps, Stella is a talented singer/songwriter who has scored with hits including "I Want to Hold You in My Dreams Tonight" and "I'm Not That Good at Goodbye."

A straw hat adorned with flowers and a price tag is the exclusive signature of famed country comedienne MINNIE PEARL. A former schoolteacher, Sarah Ophelia Colley adopted her alter ego in the 1930s and was soon a star. A member of the Grand Old Opry since 1940, she was inducted into the Country Music Hall of Fame in 1975.

CHARLEY PRIDE played semipro baseball before finding his niche in country music. Hits like "Kiss an Angel Good Morning" and "Is Anybody Going to San Antone?" have taken the Mississippi native to the top of the country charts and brought him national acclaim. He joined the Grand Ole Opry in 1993.

JEANNE PRUETT arrived in Music City in 1965 with her husband Jack, who played guitar for Marty Robbins. Her recording of "Satin Sheets" was a pop crossover success in 1973. A member of the Grand Ole Opry since 1974, she is frequently referred to as "the best cook in Nashville."

One of JERRY REED's first album titles says it all about this legendary performer: *The Unbelievable Guitar and Voice of Jerry Reed.* A master musician and songwriter, he is known for hits, including, "When You're Hot, You're Hot" and "Amos Moses." He has also starred in numerous movies, including *Smokey and the Bandit, Gator,* and *W. W. and the Dixie Dance Kings.*

DEL REEVES has been a member of the Grand Ole Opry since 1966. A native of North Carolina, his string of 1960s hits includes "Girl on the Billboard" and "Be Quiet Mind."

A former All-Pro football player for the Cincinnati Bengals, MIKE REID changed careers at the age of twenty-eight and became one of Nashville's top songwriters. His tunes include "Stranger in My House," for which he won a 1983 Grammy, "Still Losing You," and "Prisoner of the Highway." Reid scored success as a singer in 1991 with "Walk on Faith."

The RIDERS IN THE SKY—Ranger Doug, Woody Paul, and Too Slim—do things "the cowboy way." Their western-influenced country music has become a favorite of "buckeroos and buckerettes" throughout the nation.

Before "Harper Valley PTA" made JEANNIE C. RILEY an overnight sensation in 1968, she was a secretary at a Nashville record company. Her autobiography, *From Harper Valley to the Mountain Top,* traces her sudden rise to fame, the eventual disintegration of her personal and professional life, and how she rebuilt her career after embracing Christianity.

RIQUE is quite possibly Nashville's most well-known stylist. In addition to owning his own salon, he can be found behind the scenes at music video shoots, television programs, and awards shows.

BILLY JOE ROYAL became a teenage sensation in the 1960s with hits like "Down in the Boondocks" and "I Knew You When." He took a career turn to country music in the 1980s, scoring with "Out of Sight and On My Mind" and "Love Has No Right."

JOHNNY RUSSELL toiled as a top songwriter when he first came to Nashville from his native Mississippi. His song "Act Naturally" was a huge hit for Buck Owens, and later, the Beatles. His own singing career took off with hits such as "Rednecks, White Socks, and Blue Ribbon Beer" and "The Baptism of Jesse Taylor."

Country band SAWYER BROWN found fame as the first grand champions on TV's *Star Search*, hosted by Ed McMahon. Twelve years later, they continue to be one of country music's most exciting groups, fronted by lead singer Mark Miller. Their string of hits includes "Betty's Bein' Bad," "Cafe on the Corner," and "The Walk."

DAVID SCHNAUFER is the world's foremost dulcimer player. In addition to his own albums, which feature a mix of country, folk, and jazz, he has played on records with Kathy Mattea, Hank Williams, Jr., the Judds, Dan Seals, Johnny Cash, and more. He is also a member of the progressive country band, the Cactus Brothers.

EARL SCRUGGS is one of country music's premier banjo players. His partnership with the late Lester Flatt brought fame, as the duo sold more records in the 1960s for CBS than any other act except Johhny Cash. Their most popular recordings are "Foggy Mountain Breakdown" and "The Ballad of Jed Clampett," the theme from TV's *Beverly Hillbillies*. Since 1969, Scruggs has been performing with the Earl Scruggs Review.

As one-half of England Dan and John Ford Coley, DAN SEALS was one of America's biggest pop stars in the late 1970s. His career as a country superstar took off with hits like "Meet Me in Montana," "Bop," and "You Still Move Me."

A member of the Grand Ole Opry, JEANNIE SEELY made her radio debut at the age of eleven and appeared on *Midwestern Hayride* while still in high school. Once married to famed songwriter Hank Cochran, she scored hits with "Don't Touch Me" and "It's Only Love."

As a songwriter, VICTORIA SHAW has collaborated with country music's biggest star, Garth Brooks. Two of their songs, "The River" and "We Shall Be Free," helped launch her into the upper echelon of songwriting fame.

T.G. SHEPPARD (real name: Bill Browder) had a brief pop career under the name Brian Stacy in the early 1960s. He became a bona fide country star in 1974 when "Devil in the Bottle" raced to the top of the charts.

CONNIE SMITH pays homage to Roy Acuff. She fulfilled her childhood dream of performing on the Grand Old Opry when she joined the cast in 1965. Her hits include "Once a Day" and "Smooth Sailin'."

HANK SNOW, the "Singing Ranger," has been a mainstay in country music for over fifty years. A native of Liverpool, Nova Scotia, he was elected to the Country Music Hall of Fame in 1979 and is best known for the songs "I've Been Everywhere" and "I'm Movin' On."

The versatility of RAY STEVENS is demonstrated by comic songs such as "It's Me Again, Margaret" and "The Streak" and by tender ballads, including "Everything Is Beautiful." A native of Mississippi, he operates a theater in Branson, Missouri, where he enjoys playing golf when not performing.

MARTY STUART left his hometown of Philadelphia, Mississippi, at the age of thirteen to join the band of legendary Lester Flatt. He also toured with Johnny Cash before embarking on his own solo career. Hits like "Hillbilly Rock" and "Tempted" have made him one of country music's most popular stars of the 1990s.

At the suggestion of pop diva Dionne Warwick, B.J. THOMAS was handpicked by Burt Bacharach and Hal David to sing "Raindrops Keep Fallin' on My Head" for the film *Butch Cassidy and the Sundance Kid.* The 1970 hit launched Thomas on a career that continues into the 1990s, as he concentrates on contemporary Christian music.

HANK THOMPSON made his debut as Hank the Hired Hand on a local radio show while still a schoolboy. An auspicious debut for the Texas native, who was elected to the Country Music Hall of Fame in 1989.

TANYA TUCKER, the "Texas Tornado," made her country music debut at the age of thirteen with "Delta Dawn" in 1972. Nineteen years later, she was named Female Vocalist of the Year by the Country Music Association. The mother of two children, she is also a champion in cutting horse competitions.

PORTER WAGONER is renowned as country music's ambassador to the world. An early star on *Ozark Jubilee* in Springfield, Missouri, he found national success with his own syndicated television program, *The Porter Wagoner Show,* in which he tapped a then-aspiring young singer named Dolly Parton to be his duet partner.

When country music singers need advice about what to wear and what image to project, at one time or another they're sure to call VANESSA WARE. A professional clothing designer and image consultant for the past thirty-one years, her clients include Wynonna Judd, Suzy Bogguss, Lorrie Morgan, and Martina McBride. She discovered her passion for costuming as a teenager, while serving as an apprentice at the Stratford Shakespeare Festival.

KEVIN WELCH has been called the best country lyricist to emerge since Steve Earle. His songs have been recorded by Gary Morris, the Judds, Moe Bandy, Don Williams, and scores of others. The Oklahoma singer/songwriter has found a huge following in Europe, and he can also be seen in Music City performing with his band, the Overtones.

KITTY WELLS has reigned as the "Queen of Country Music" since her 1952 hit "It Wasn't God Who Made Honky Tonk Angels." Married to singer Johnny Wright, the Tennessee native was elected to the Country Music Hall of Fame in 1976 and has been a member of the Grand Ole Opry for over forty years.

WILD ROSE, composed of Pam Gadd, Wanda Vick, Nancy Given-Prout, and Kathy Mac, is one of the most successful all-female bands in history. Their country/bluegrass stylings have made them extremely popular in Europe, where they appear in countless festivals each year.

Since 1972, DON WILLIAMS has been known as the "Gentle Giant" to country music fans. The soft-spoken performer, voted Male Vocalist of the Year by the Country Music Association in 1978, is known for hits such as "Amanda," "Tulsa Time," and "Some Broken Hearts Never Mend." He remains one of country music's most popular performers in both the United States and England.

BOXCAR WILLIE was born Lecil Travis Martin in Sterratt, Texas. A former disk jockey, he adopted his now-famous persona in 1975 and found stardom in the United Kingdom at the prestigious Wembley Festival. A member of the Grand Old Opry, he was also the first entertainer to buy his own theater in the country music boomtown of Branson, Missouri.

When softspoken KELLY WILLIS sings, her distinctive voice fills the room with emotion. One of country music's progressive new breed of singers, she has scored with hits like "Baby Take a Piece of My Heart" and "The Heart That Love Forgot."

After finding monumental success in her native Canada, MICHELLE WRIGHT headed for Nashville in 1991 and has become one of country music's most popular new stars. Songs like "New Kind of Love" and "Take It Like a Man" have endeared her to country fans across the United States.

TRISHA YEARWOOD set country music on its ear in 1991 when her debut single, "She's in Love with the Boy," went flying to the top of the charts. Two platinum albums—*Trisha Yearwood* and *Hearts in Armor*—later, the Georgia native is hailed as one of country music's most talented vocalists.

INDEX